The
Equipping the Saints
Series

Book Two

Change Your Mind
~
Prepare Your Mind for Action

By
Michael E. Wolfe

TABLE OF CONTENTS

Acknowledgements

It is obviously appropriate to begin by acknowledging the triune God for the great and wonderful way He has designed and created human beings; for the truly incredible capacities He has given us. In light of the dreadful misuse of such capacities it is only appropriate to express utmost gratitude for His tremendous provision to save and transform human beings and the human race and for the impact His provision and presence has personally had upon me. In the process the Lord used an extended number of *people* to open my eyes to His provision, presence and truth. Some of them with which I have ongoing, personal relationship, some are acquaintances, some I have never met and all of them to whom I am grateful.

I would first like to thank my wife, Deb, for her prayers, influence and companionship without which my life would most certainly be dreadful on a number of levels. I am grateful to my brother-in-law, Randall Davis, for the role he played in my conversion and for guidance in the development of my Biblical understanding. The discipleship course I developed, have been teaching for years and upon which this series of books is based is the result of a pattern he employed in a series of evangelistic meetings for which he spoke, that pattern being Change Your Heart, Change Your Mind, Change Your Life, Change the World. I have gotten many miles out of this. As well, the following list of people is, in large part, the result of guidance I received from him early in my Christian life. I would like to acknowledge the labors and teachings of six specific people who have had the most direct impact upon my growth and ministry. Gordon Olson, Harry Conn, Paris Reidhead, Charles Finney, Winkie Pratney and Dean Harvey are men whose love for God and love of truth have blessed me many times over. The information you will find in the pages of this book are largely the result of establishing a Biblical perspective as a result of teaching and clarification gained from those listed above.

Finally, I can only close by saying that I believe that this acknowledgement is very incomplete. So many others have played roles of importance throughout my life are not mentioned by name. Many have prayed for, fellowshipped with, encouraged and supported me throughout the years. To them I apologize and state that your goodness is appreciated and will surely be rewarded in far greater ways than an acknowledgement in a book that will likely spend its existence in obscurity.

Foreword

It is my privilege to recommend this book to all. Michael describes the contents as "foundational information." This is certainly true. As I read the manuscript, I was reminded of the passage in Hebrews 5:12-12.

> "For though by this time you ought to be teachers, you need someone to teach you again the first principles of the oracles of God; and you have come to need milk and not solid food. For everyone who partakes only of milk is unskilled in the word of righteousness, for he is a babe. But solid food belongs to those who are of full age, that is, those who by reason of use have their senses exercised to discern both good and evil."

The sad fact is that the "foundational information" in this book would be described as "milk" by the writer of Hebrews, and yet many Christians today do not know these necessary truths.

As Michael has developed each item of this "foundational information." they have been treated as "solid food" as it is understood in the book of Hebrews. He treats each item in a comprehensive way, so that it will benefit everyone who takes the time, not only to read, but to think through what he has said. The author's experience as a pastor, a teacher of prisoners in jail, and as a teacher of young people in Youth With A Mission (YWAM), has given him the practical experience to speak with authority on these subjects, which are normally so neglected in the body of Christ.

One point that he makes very strongly is that much of the teaching we hear is so strong against works that it often discourages obedience, and serves to encourage

Christians to make light of sin. Here is a quote: *"It is common among certain Christian communities to emphasize that we are not saved by works. This is frequently communicated in such a way that one might get the impression that behavior and obedience are unimportant or they are a form of self-righteousness to be avoided at all cost."* If this is received wrongly by a Christian, it could lead him to be lax in obedience to the Lord.

My background in the Pentecostal church has given me certain instances where the emotions and feelings are emphasized over rationality. I like that he emphasizes that "God created human beings with a mind designed after His own mind." Praise the Lord. Our minds are not as good as God's, but they function in the same way, therefore we can "reason together" and we can really have conversations with God. Additionally, Michael very wisely defines Biblical love.

Now that I have read the first two books of this series, which will ultimately comprise four books, I could recommend to every Christian pastor to use these books as texts in a "foundational" class for Christians. - Dr. Dean H. Harvey

Dean H, Harvey has served the Lord in ministry for 62 years. He was licensed by t he Assemblies of God in July of 1954, and has followed a dual career path, serving in the Navy until his retirement in 1971, while also filling pastoral positions at the same time. He and his wife, Shirley, has pioneered one church, and pastored full time for 37 years until his wife became sick and required them to move to a warmer climate.

Dean attended Central Bible College in Springfield, Missouri, and after retirement from the Navy, completed his BA in Christian Counseling from Valley Christian University in Fresno, California. In 2011 he received an honorary PhD from Southern California Christian College in Rancho Mirage, California.

In addition to his pastoral ministry, Dean has been teaching in Youth With A Mission (YWAM) schools since 1954, pioneering the School of the Bible in Tyler, Texas in 1982. He has written two books, Ransom. The High Cost of Sin and Pastor, What About Judas?, and has another, What Kind of People?, which will be published early in 2016.

Introduction

Perspective is tremendously important. In my previous book, Change Your Heart, the focus was on one's ultimate purpose or goal in life. Each human being has a supreme purpose or object of pursuit. This is either something one embraces by "default," without consciously, intelligently evaluating what the ultimate motive behind all else is, or it is strategically and analytically chosen. Regarding the issue of the heart, the bottom-line is that there are only two options – everyone does what they do, either to please God supremely or to please Self supremely. If you desire further clarification, I suggest you read the previous book.

Once an individual establishes an ultimate motive, all else becomes a manifestation of this heart. In regard to the mind of man, there are two important initial considerations. First, our heart exercises an influence on what we think about and how we use / govern our minds. One whose genuine goal in life is to please God will be inclined to think differently than one intent on pleasing Self. Secondly, our mind is affected because we are engaged in a process of learning what pleases God and understanding the principles of righteous, kingdom living. In other words, one's heart affects what flows *from* the mind and what flows *into* the mind.

It is very important to realize that this should not be seen as an automatic process. We are to actively endeavor to govern our mental processes if we are to experience positive growth and maturity. We must be concerned not only with *what* we think but *how* we think. That being said, this book is not about *how* to think, how to understand and employ laws of logic and use one's reasoning powers. There are many significant books available on laws of logic and how to apply them. In Change Your Mind you will find a presentation of certain concepts that I have found to be foundational and helpful for understanding God, His kingdom and introductory ideas about the fact that man is created in His image.

In the first chapter, we will consider certain distinctions related to the modes of government God has established in regard to His involvement with creation, specifically focusing on His government over the human race.

Chapter two reflects upon the relationship between being exposed to truth, gaining understanding of the truth to which one is exposed and acting upon such truth. Again, the process of growing in understanding and loving God with all our minds is not an automatic arrangement, it is one that requires very specific attention.

In chapter three we consider the nature of moral agency as a foundation to understanding the nature of love. There seems to be a void in understanding and appreciating this topic in contemporary culture and, consequently, a significant amount of confusion which leads to various difficulties and complications on very practical levels.

Moving into chapter four we give attention to insight related to the role the lust of the flesh, the lust of the eye and the pride of life play in spiritual warfare. Awareness of the enemies strategy is helpful in avoiding deception and defeat.

Finally, the emphasis of the fifth chapter is on the holistic nature of the Christian faith as we consider what Luke 2:52 tells us about the growth experience of Jesus. In this passage we find four broad categories of life in which we are told that Jesus experienced increase. Recognizing the truth of this statement about His incarnate experience, we make application to our human experience, especially in reference to those who are followers of Jesus.

It is my hope that this humble effort to present foundational information about the importance of our mental perspective and the role the mind plays in gaining understanding will encourage you to "prepare your minds for action" (1 Pe.1:13).

~

"If God desired to have moral creatures in His universe, He could only have them by endowing them with free will, the power to accept or reject His own will. The determination to create moral beings was a determination to create those who should be the cause of their own actions, and who might set aside His own laws."
Dr. Robert Flint, Theism (William Blackwood and Sons), p.255, quoted from Providence, Prayer and Power (see below)

"The God of providence rules and overrules, but He does not by His omnipotence overpower and override and destroy man's true freedom of will. Things that are do not, as they are, represent God's perfect providence, but rather reflect His providence as affected by human free agency and as marred by man's sin."
Wilbur Fisk Tillett, Providence, Prayer and Power (Cokesbury Press), p.28

~

Chapter One

Concerning God and His Government over His Creation

God created the heavens and the earth. God, an eternal, personal, Being designed, created and governs our universe. As part of this design, God employs varied and appropriate means to govern different aspects of His creation. When considering such arrangements, it is particularly important that we gain insight into God's mode of government applicable to human beings. Doing so involves making appropriate distinctions between physical law and moral law, between the government of physical creation, the government of animal & plant life and the government of beings endowed with moral agency.[1] As we become familiar with God's design for governing the human race, we must resolve to honor it if we expect to produce good results.

Classes of Creation

A portion of God's creation possesses life but is void of moral agency. This order of creation is **animate (having life), non-moral (not to be confused with immoral) creation**. God also created many things that have neither life nor moral agency. These are known as **inanimate (without life), non-moral creation**. Along with the two categories mentioned above, He created beings that have both life and moral agency. We refer to this as **animate, moral creation**. With each class of creation, God arranged for an appropriate mode of government. Within

---

[1] A moral agent is one possessing an intellectual ability to perceive moral obligation, a conscience to measure moral accountability, sensibility (an emotional structure capable of sensing virtue and blame), and free will; those capable of discerning and choosing between good and evil, right and wrong.

each area of creation, there are very deep and fascinating discoveries one might make. Though there are marvelous aspects to each realm of creation, the goal of this chapter is to understand important truths about the design of human beings and the form of Divine government to which we are subject.

Animate, Non-moral Creation

Animate, non-moral creation consists of vertebrate and invertebrate animal life as well as various forms of vegetation. Among the long list within this category are such familiar things as canine, feline, cattle, reptile, sea creatures, birds, insects, trees, flowers, grass, fungus, etc. Within each class referred to above (and more) there are overwhelmingly tremendous varieties, variations and subdivisions. The two common characteristics of everything in this realm of creation are, they possess some form of **life,** and they *do not* possess **moral capabilities**. For our purposes, we will briefly consider the twofold division of animal and vegetable life.

It is helpful to consider the distinction between impulse, instinct and direct Divine intervention as we think of God's mode of government for the *animal* kingdom. Impulse refers to certain internal drives, urges, appetites or desires that relate to food, sexual / reproductive activity, shelter / protection, survival, etc. This area is more basic than the area of instinct in that many different animals share similar *impulses* but are equipped with distinct *instincts* regarding the way they respond to or satisfy such impulses. The instinct of a lion is considerably different from the instinct of a hummingbird when it comes to satisfying the impulse (appetite) to eat. They share a common impulse related to hunger, but very different instincts for satisfying their hunger. Both, the impulse and the instinct, are important aspects of the mode of government established by their Creator. Investigating the tremendous variety of instincts in operation throughout the animal kingdom is a fascinating study that reflects the creativity and wisdom of God, but we will not pursue such an investigation at this time. Finally, we have evidence, particularly within the Biblical record, that God is able, and sometimes willing, to override or set aside the normal function of the impulses and instincts of animals, exercising direct Divine intervention. Scripture provides a number of examples. Hungry lions did not eat Daniel; ravens delivered food to Elijah; a donkey spoke to Balaam, etc. Though God has a standard that consistently applies to specific creatures, He has the ability to dynamically and actively alter the normal mode of operation and act in a miraculous manner.[2] When, how and why He does so is an investigation we will currently forego.

Within the realm of *vegetation*, we find a mode of operation that is quite fascinating. The life form and function of this realm are considerably different from the animal kingdom. However, they display patterns and characteristics that provide for their continued existence. The animate activity of vegetation is likely more complex and intriguing than we generally suspect. Again, without delving into detail, we find an arrangement that speaks of God's design and mode of government for this particular realm of creation.

The realms of creation referred to above are not equipped with moral faculties. The mode of government applicable to that existing in the animate, non-moral realm (both animal and vegetable) excludes the use of analytical reasoning and moral choice.

---

[2] A miracle, by definition, involves operating outside the normal, established physical law applicable to a certain realm of creation. As such, the miraculous can never become the norm or it ceases to be miraculous.

Imagine two hungry dogs and two bowls of food. In the process of being fed, it is stated, in a simple, matter-of-fact manner, that the first bowl of food placed in front of them is for Fluffy. Rover is told to wait patiently until the second bowl is prepared and placed on the floor. Would such a calm, thoughtful declaration inspire Rover to consider his moral obligation to avoid diving headfirst into the bowl placed upon the floor? The instinct of both hungry dogs would inspire an active endeavor to eat. The effort to secure the food for their own personal consumption might even inspire them to become aggressive. Rover does not engage in moral evaluation about whether he should or should not eat from the bowl containing Fluffy's food. If there had been prior *conditioning* one might manage to modify Rover's behavior to some degree. Modifications made due to conditioning are not the same as moral choice. It is worth noting that even in the famous experiments performed by Ivan Pavlov, not all dogs responded to efforts to condition them. As well, it was acknowledged that the results of his experiments were not to be applied to human beings.[3] Soon, we will consider how the issue of hunger, as mentioned above, applies when speaking of two human beings.

As the purpose of the current information is merely introductory, we will not consider the massive amount of detail available in reference to such issues but instead turn our attention to the realm of inanimate, non-moral creation.

Inanimate, Non-moral Creation

In the realm of inanimate, non-moral creation, we have such things as rocks, waterways, planets and other aspects of physical creation that are void of life and incapable of choice and the associated processes. When

---

[3] Albert H. Hobbs, Man is Moral Choice (New York: Arlington House Publishers), p.134-135, 177-178

considering the overwhelming complexity of the universe, being tremendously impressed and awestruck is a proper reaction. From the incomprehensible vastness of our galaxy (and others) to molecular structures that are invisible to the naked eye, we are surrounded by the wonders of God's inanimate, non-moral creation. In reference to our previous realm of creation (animate, non-moral creation), we recognized the significance of built-in instinct and impulse that play a role in the governance of its behavior. Inanimate, non-moral creation is void of such instinct and impulse. This realm is governed by standing laws of nature that act *upon* the physical dimensions of our universe. A common example is the law of gravity. God has designed that such physical laws are instrumental for governing this realm of creation. The orbit and rotation of planets depend neither upon an internal impulse nor upon choices they must make. The operation of such laws has a cause and effect relationship with the entity in question. We have no record of God saying to planet earth, "I set before you today rotating or not rotating, orbiting or not orbiting so choose..."

Along with the considerations above, Scripture reveals that God has the ability, and sometimes chooses, to override, manipulate or set aside the laws of nature. We generally refer to such events as miraculous or supernatural. To this point, we can see that the government of God over inanimate, non-moral creation is distinct from animate, non-moral creation, and we shall see that both of the aforementioned are distinct from animate, moral creation.

Again, we will take our investigation no further but encourage the reader to consider the marvelous complexity that is available when studying inanimate, non-moral creation.

Animate, Moral Creation

The previous categories of creation have been given a much more shallow treatment than they could have been given as the current category is of primary interest for our present purposes. Within this realm, we will consider God's governmental interaction with the human race.[4] The phrase "animate, moral creation" would indicate an order of creation that has life (animate) and possesses capacities and abilities to evaluate, gain knowledge of and choose between right and wrong (moral). Though the mysteries and intrigue of biological[5] life are truly astounding, the focus of our current study will be the *moral* dimension of man. We will consider the means by which God has arranged to govern in the affairs of man.

The Divine government associated with animate, moral creation involves two important sub-divisions. One consists of overseeing human beings as they freely employ their God-given capacities and abilities while the other considers God's interactions that override, limit or simply do not involve man's free use of his God-given capacities and abilities. The first is referred to as Moral Government while the second is commonly discussed under the heading of Providential Government.[6]

---

[4] It is conceivable that this realm would also apply to the angelic order but this subject will not be considered in the current work.

[5] It is worth emphasizing that maintaining a distinction between physical / biological functions and moral actions is of great importance. One might notice that modern psychology (the study of the soul) is notorious for violating this distinction. Though the two realms have various levels of interaction, their distinct nature must be recognized. Moral choices can have an effect upon the physical / biological realm and the physical realm can be an influential factor in one's moral choice, but great harm is done when blurring the lines between these two distinct aspects of created order.

[6] The phrase "providential government" is, in my estimation, insufficient for the form of government it is intended to define. Not having identified a new phrase, I will continue to use it, along with the

Moral Government

This form of Divine government is applicable to beings (human beings, in particular) designed with a mind capable of analyzing and understanding moral law /obligation, otherwise, able to distinguish between right and wrong.[7] Along with the capability to understand moral obligation, is the ability to choose between obedience and disobedience. The law describes moral obligation, and the positive consequences associated with obedience and negative consequences associated with disobedience. The law has no power or ability within it to help a moral agent achieve obedience, but it does provide a motivating factor; it is influential, not causative. Moral government employs various influences designed to encourage and secure right moral choice. Every form of influence in the Divine moral government is intended to encourage proper moral behavior and / or discourage improper moral behavior. The influences of moral government are *sufficient* to produce right moral action but do not *cause* such action. Though the influences and guidance of a moral governor be perfect, the subject of moral government has the responsibility to use his or her moral capabilities to originate one's own *purpose* and *action* – one's own internal and external response. The subject of moral government (the moral agent) has the power to cooperate with or to suppress, resist and / or reject moral influence, even perfect moral influence. A moral agent is free to choose right or wrong moral action and is, therefore, accountable for the response he or she originates. The wrong moral choice of a subject of God's moral government cannot be blamed on God, as His guidance is

---

phrase "providential intervention," to refer to a governmental system of cause and effect.

[7] Right and wrong, in this sense, is not simply a reference to *factual* information, as in mathematics, but to *morally* right and morally wrong purposes, plans and actions.

always sufficient to produce right moral behavior. Such a governmental system is always consistent with the capacities and abilities of the moral agent.

The above, brief description of this realm of Divine government over man is natural to the Biblical text. In fact, it is difficult to read Scripture reasonably without recognizing the existence of this arrangement. We could engage in an extensive evaluation of texts but will simply look at Deuteronomy 30:15-20 as a representative passage.

> "See, I have set before you today life and prosperity, and death and adversity; in that I command you today to love the Lord your God, to walk in His ways and to keep His commandments and His statutes and His judgments, that you may live and multiply, and that the Lord your God may bless you in the land where you are entering to possess it. But if your heart turns away and you will not obey, but are drawn away and worship other gods and serve them, I declare to you today that you shall surely perish. You shall not prolong your days in the land where you are crossing the Jordan to enter and possess it. I call heaven and earth to witness against you today, that I have set before you life and death, the blessing and the curse. So choose life in order that you may live, you and your descendants, by loving the Lord your God, by obeying His voice, and by holding fast to Him; for this is your life and the length of your days, that you may live in the land which the Lord swore to your fathers, to Abraham, Isaac, and Jacob, to give them."

This is a statement from God to the Israelites by way of Moses. Though it has a particular historical and cultural context, there are standing truths and principles that have application to human beings in general. Such truths are the ones to which I intend to draw attention. First, there are two, and only two, ultimate options placed before the people receiving this information. With each ultimate choice, Moses states the positive and negative outcome. It is very important that we distinguish between ultimate choice and the product or outcome of ultimate choice.[8] The positive product of one ultimate choice is life, prosperity and blessing. The negative product of the other ultimate choice is death, adversity and curse. I use the word product because life, death, prosperity, adversity, blessing and curse cannot be chosen directly. They come into existence as the result of a prior choice. The ultimate choice that produces life, prosperity and blessing is "to love the Lord your God, to walk in His ways and to keep His commandments and His statutes and His judgments." The ultimate choice that produces death, adversity and curse is turning one's heart from God, not obeying His commandments, worshiping and serving other gods. God, through Moses, informs us of the right choice ("…choose life…*by* loving the Lord your God, *by* obeying His voice, *by* holding fast to Him…"). It is, as well, quite obvious that human beings have the ability to understand the ideas communicated by these words and the ability to make the choice we are told that we should make. If one should doubt that we have the ability needed

---

[8] This distinction has tremendous significance in reference to the issue of repentance, conversion and salvation. Though there are a multitude of influences, experiences and ingredients in the process leading up to the point of repentance, the ultimate, climactic decision made in repentance is to LOVE GOD supremely. The decision is not to choose life, blessing, reward, heaven, salvation, happiness, freedom, etc. as entities in and of themselves. Everything associated with salvation (such as the list above) is the product of having a right relationship with God characterized by our love for Him becoming the supreme motivating factor in our lives. It is very clear in the Deuteronomy text that one can experience life, prosperity and blessing "…*by* **loving the Lord your God, by obeying His voice, and by holding fast to Him.**"

to meet the requirements of God, a verse prior to the passage quoted should eliminate this doubt. Verse 11 reads, "For this commandment which I command you today is not too difficult for you, nor is it out of reach."[9] Moral guilt is a matter of "will not" in contrast to "cannot." The elements of this passage provide us with a clear example of moral government. We see communication about right and wrong, about the outcome of each, as well as encouragement and motivation to choose right. It is also important to recognize that right moral standing is not merely related to external activity but depends upon the internal motive from which external activity originates ("...by *loving* the Lord your God...").

Returning to an earlier illustration, we can consider the case of two normal, hungry men. Imagine placing a wonderful platter of food on a table, telling Bill the platter is for Bob, and stating that he must wait patiently while his platter is prepared. Does Bill have the ability to understand the meaning of the words spoken? Does he have the ability to cooperate with the requirement of the words spoken, even when experiencing hunger? Does he have the ability to disregard, though he understands, the requirement of the words spoken? We should be able to see the difference between this scenario when it involves dogs (animate, non-moral creation) and when it involves human beings (animate, moral creation).

As we prepare to turn our attention to the nature of Providential Government, we will clarify the basic nature of this form of government, and then consider its relationship with and distinction from Moral Government. It is my conviction that careful thinking in reference to these two modes of government will affect our theology in

---

[9] Regarding moral obligation and accountability, God requires that we live up to the truth and ability we possess. As a way to help students grasp this concept I often ask, "Can you throw a baseball as far as you can throw a baseball?"

tremendously important, foundational ways. Our theology, then, *should* inform our practice. In keeping with the purpose of this book, Change Your Mind, I suggest that our understanding of the distinct realms and forms of Divine government will aid in preventing imbalance and error in our Biblical reading and theological studies. Attempting to make all of Scripture fit into only one category has resulted in much of the error, tension and confusion we have seen in theology and doctrine.

Providential Government

Concerning this mode of Divine government, I will distinguish between a concept of providence as *provisional* (provision and response) and a concept that is more in the realm of *causative* (cause and effect). I have been attempting to identify a better phrase for the cause and effect mode as "providential government" does not, in my opinion, best suit this category.

The first dimension of providential government under consideration regards God employing His intelligence and power to *provide* everything necessary for human beings, individually and corporately, to produce good, healthy, balanced outcome. In reference to this category, it is helpful to think of the word providence as "provide-ence." Such provision actually *lays the foundation* for moral government. Man's original design, all the abilities and capacities possessed, are providential. Human beings did not choose to have such abilities though we must choose what we will do with them. What man does with such abilities and capacities is associated with man as a moral agent or as a subject of moral government. Beyond this, God providentially arranges for redemptive options designed for man's recovery from improper use of his moral agency. Such provision is conceived of and made by God (providential government) but produces no positive result unless responded to properly by those for whom the provision applies (moral government). The provisions are made for the promotion of the highest good possible, but they do not guarantee, secure or cause the highest good to come into existence. To expand on this idea, I quote from N. W. Taylor, who states, "The acts therefore of giving a law, sustaining its authority by sanctions, providing means of conveying truth to the mind, are not constituent parts of moral government, but are *providential* acts which are necessary to that *influence* which constitutes moral government."[10]

Genesis 1:26[11] reveals that God made necessary provision for humans to be distinct. What man does with the created design, abilities, capacities and capabilities provided by God is another discussion. God, in His provide-ence, created human beings in His own image with specific abilities, created an environment full of resources with which we are to interact and gave us the responsibility of stewardship over creation for which we are held accountable.

We now shift our attention to the concept of providential government that is associated with cause and effect. It is concerning this concept that I believe the phrase "providential government" could be replaced with a more appropriate phrase. However, not having a better phrase, I will proceed to explain the concept.

According to this concept, Scripture supplies us with examples of God, not simply making a provision but overriding or setting aside man's moral agency in order to

---

[10] N. W. Taylor, Lecture on the Moral Government of God, Vol. II, (New York: Clark, Austin & Smith), p.298; Michigan Historical Reprint Series

[11] "Then God said, 'Let Us make man in Our image, according to Our likeness; and let them rule over the fish of the sea and over the birds of the sky and over the cattle and over all the earth, and over every creeping thing that creeps on the earth…'"

accomplish something of importance. In the animate and inanimate, non-moral realm, God is free and able to set aside the normal instincts or laws that are associated with such modes of government. In the exercise of providential government, God can, consistent with His character, set aside man's normal moral freedom when He sees fit. When moral government is intact, the moral agent is accountable for the choices and actions produced. On occasions when God supersedes man's moral freedom, the issues of man's accountability (good or bad) ceases to be a factor. That God intervenes in this way is sure defensible on a Biblical basis. How to discern when such intervention has taken place in extra-Biblical accounts, throughout human history, is challenging. This mode of governmental interaction with the human race is not intended to be the norm. Even if it, at times, becomes the status quo, it is not the norm.

Summary

In light of the two concepts considered above, one might say that providential government establishes the foundation of moral government. In other words, God providentially created moral beings and chose, consequently, to establish moral government. It must also be acknowledged that, at times, providential government *supersedes* moral government. As we study Scripture in an effort to understand God, His kingdom and His relationship with creation (including man), it is important to maintain distinctions and balance regarding the different forms of government. We err if we attempt to make our understanding of God's interaction with creation fit into only one of the modes of government to which I have referred. If we isolate certain providential acts of God and assume this is His only mode of governance, we will misunderstand and misrepresent reality. If, on the other hand, we only acknowledge accounts that involve freedom of choice and contingency, we will fail to represent reality effectively. We must also recognize that there is often overlap between the various modes of interaction in which God engages with creation.

God's interaction with Pharaoh provides a great case study in the interactions of both providential and moral government when studied with appropriate sensitivity. Exodus 11:10 states that, "…the Lord hardened Pharaoh's heart, and he did not let the sons of Israel go out of his land."[12] Though I do not intend to delve into the details of the preceding verse, I will clarify that God's activity, described above, is not related to Pharaoh's moral accountability or salvation. It refers to God strengthening Pharaoh in the resolve that Pharaoh had previously established in his effort to resist God and prevent Israel from leaving Egypt at a time when the pressure became too great for him to carry out his intention. The following verses provide insight into the reason why God did this.

"…I will harden Pharaoh's heart that I may multiply My signs and My wonders in the land of Egypt." (Exodus 7:3, NASB)

"…for this cause I have allowed you to remain, in order to show you My power, and in order to proclaim My name through all the earth." (Exodus 9:16, NASB)

"…I have hardened his heart and the heart of his servants, that I may perform these signs of Mine among them…" (Exodus 10:1, NASB)

---

[12] Also see Dt.2:25; Josh.11:20; I Ki.22:19-23; Ps.22:28; 66:7; Pr.21:1; Jer.32:27-30; 50:9; Da.4:17, 32; Zeph.3:8; Jn.7:30; 18:31, 32; 19:9-11; Ro.13:1; Re.17:17

God clearly intended to display His power through signs and wonders, and it appears that He was not going to stop until He had "defeated" the false gods of Egypt. Why did God want to do this?

> "...I will harden Pharaoh's heart, and he will chase after them; and I will be honored through Pharaoh and all his army, and the Egyptians will know that I am the Lord." (Exodus 14:4, NASB; also see Ex.7:5 and 14:17, 18)

God wanted to bolster the confidence of the Israelites as they faced the outrageous challenge of venturing into the destitute wilderness of the dessert land (Ex.14:31) *and* as well, impress the Egyptians with the truth that He is Lord (Ex.14:18).

Application

Having briefly sketched the previous distinctions, we can now consider the importance thereof. The comprehension of the components of moral government provides a sufficient foundation for understanding man's moral responsibility and accountability. Such understanding is instrumental in the development of healthy individuals and society. Following are brief sections that encourage the reader to exercise caution in formulating an understanding of man's relationship with God and with God's creation. This is not simply an exercise in theory but also an effort to promote the fact that the understanding from which we shape our practical approach toward life must not be taken lightly.

Concerning Moral Government and the Government of Animate, Non-moral Creation

As I minister within the walls of the local prison, I recognize that people are incarcerated, in part, because of allowing their fleshly impulses to rule their behavior. Failing to distinguish between the created design of animal life and the created design of human beings (moral agents) is one very important ingredient in this scenario. For some, this provides the false justification and inspiration for operating according to their impulses, "instincts" and sensual desires. They yield to and are governed by such desires instead of exercising rational control over them. Becoming aware of this distinction often proves to be a source of significant enlightenment for those interested in finding freedom from past patterns. Doing what is needed to get free from the bondage incurred due to a lifestyle cultivated on this error is another issue altogether. Darwinism, and modern, secular psychology, in great measure, have contributed to the strengthening of this destructive misconception even among those who do not explicitly or knowingly ascribe to the beliefs postulated by such. Human beings, having been created in the image of God, have been equipped with certain capabilities that we must learn to use properly. Any or all such capabilities can be used properly or improperly. Having incorrect assumptions in these matters has often discouraged healthy development of one's moral capacities. As an individual purposes to be pleasing to God[13] and gains understanding of God's governmental design for moral agents, he or she can begin to honor this design and produce good fruit.

Some people are inclined to view all of life through a version of providential government, often referring to it as "sovereignty," and deny the idea that God can providentially arrange to establish a moral government and grant the human race genuine moral freedom. I concur with N. W. Taylor who wrote, "It is the philosophical doctrine

---

[13] See my previous book, "Change Your Heart."

of some theologians, that all events are brought to pass by the direct efficiency of God; in other words, that neither matter nor mind possesses efficiency in itself or is in its own nature an efficient cause, but that all material phenomena and mental acts are results of divine efficiency, as directly and truly as the existence of any created thing. To this philosophical doctrine, in its full extent at least, I cannot subscribe."[14]

It is also important to note that a proper understanding of "fallen" man, though a horrible condition, still recognizes human beings as human beings (moral agents). A human being is not an animal even when he or she foolishly chooses to act like one. Neither are we organic machines, as a naturalistic worldview and many of the behavioral "sciences" would suggest. Human beings, even in a fallen state, are beings that have been created in the image of God. We can dishonor and violate this image, but it is, nonetheless, the image in which we have been created.

Concerning Moral Good and Moral Evil

Recognizing the distinction between moral law/government and physical law is important on many levels. It is, as well, significant to realize how such distinctions affect us in practical ways. The "influence and response" aspect of moral law/government must be kept separate from the "cause and effect" aspect of physical law. This being the case, I would like to address the concept of *producing fruit*.

In the account given of God creating the physical universe, we read in Genesis 1:11-12, "Then God said, 'Let the earth sprout vegetation, plants yielding seed, and fruit

---

[14] N. W. Taylor, Lecture on the Moral Government of God, Vol. II, (New York: Clark, Austin & Smith), p.307; Michigan Historical Reprint Series

trees bearing fruit after their kind, with seed in them, on the earth'; and it was so. And the earth brought forth vegetation, plants yielding seed after their kind, and trees bearing fruit, with seed in them, after their kind; and God saw that it was good." Notice the inbuilt procedure of "bearing fruit after their kind." On the physical level, plants produce other plants "after their kind," animals produce other animals "after their kind" and the human species produces human species "after their kind."

As we carefully consider the moral application of a similar procedure, we find certain interesting insights with which it is worth wrestling. First, we cannot simply say that a righteous man (or woman) will automatically produce righteous offspring "after their kind." However, a righteous person will exercise an influence that *tends to* produce "fruit after their kind." Again, this is not the "cause and effect" procedure seen in the physical realm. We can see this concept referred to and dealt with in a passage such as Ezekiel 18.

The next dimension to consider regarding the moral dynamic of producing "fruit" involves the challenge of cleansing what is impure in comparison to defiling what is pure. Consider the prophetic[15] proclamation found in Haggai 2:11-13, "Thus says the Lord of hosts, 'Ask now the priests for a ruling: If a man carries holy meat in the fold of his garment, and touches bread with this fold, or cooked food, wine, oil, or any other food, will it become holy?' And the priests answered and said, 'No.' Then Haggai said, 'If one who is unclean from a corpse touches any of these, will the latter become unclean?' And the priests answered and said, 'It will become unclean.'" The basic emphasis in this statement is that it is easier to *produce* defilement than to *cleanse and correct* defilement. Touching something unclean with something clean does

---

[15] This use of "prophetic" is simply in reference to spiritually and morally insightful analysis.

not produce cleansing. Touching something clean with something unclean does produce defilement. This is a physical analogy that, when applied to man's moral condition, must be handled with appropriate sensitivity and care. Neither the morally defiled nor the morally pure are automatically altered by *exposure* to one another. However, it appears, by the intention of these words and by practical experience, that, sadly, it is more challenging for the morally pure to produce "fruit after their kind" than for the morally impure to produce "fruit after their kind."[16]

Recognizing this fact, sheds very intense light on God's reaction in Genesis 6:5-6 where it reads, "Then the Lord saw that the wickedness of man was great on the earth, and that every intent of the thoughts of his heart was only evil continually. And the Lord was sorry that He had made man on the earth, and He was grieved in His heart." God did not take man's condition and the challenge of restoring humanity from his great defilement lightly. The rapid, downward spiral that entangles individuals, families (as godly, righteous leadership and authority give way to selfish irresponsibility), institutions and nations is much more powerful than most people realize. Two extremes tend to pervert and misrepresent the reality and intensity of the spread of *moral* evil. One extreme removes the concept of sin and evil from the realm of moral agency by suggesting or overtly claiming that the entire human race became guilty and sinful as an automatic result of Adam's sin. The other lowers the bar regarding the nature of sin and wickedness by accepting sinful behavior as relatively normal human conduct because it has become the status quo. In both aforementioned cases, little effort is made to combat the ravages of sin. To deal with the presence of sin,

---

[16] This is not an indictment against the morally pure regarding their impotence or inability but rather a commentary on the *responses* to the efforts and influences of the morally pure as they "touch" the world around them.

we must make a serious effort to understand the type of moral wickedness with which we are actually dealing; the type of entanglement that manifests itself as society breaks down and disintegrates. I am amazed when seeing pockets of people within the church assuming that simply "touching" the unclean with a positive, uplifting message will make them clean. This type of undiscerning, immature underestimation will prove destructive and, even, deadly. Moral defilement must not be taken lightly!

Finally, it is fitting to summarize much of what has been stated in this closing section by making reference to the idea of determinism. Many people, whether carefully or haphazardly considered, have a view which assumes that God is exalted by ascribing to Him total control of all that happens in every event and circumstance. Often referred to as meticulous providence / sovereignty, this view is very difficult to defend Biblically. It leads to "explaining away" certain clear statements and teaching in Scripture. It also eliminates (though there are efforts made to say that it does not) man's moral freedom and responsibility. As well, it creates confusion about God's character as we try to understand why He would cause people to sin and then judge them for the sin He caused them to commit all the while maintaining that He is not culpable for such an arrangement.

It would be beneficial for the body of Christ to maintain a greater sensitivity to the various modes of government exercised by God. We would benefit if we were to distinguish between moral and physical law, the realm of moral government and providential government (both applicable but distinct in God's involvement in human history), and if we were to better understand and teach issues related to moral agency. Often, we are too quick to lock into a prevailing mode and evaluate everything through one limited, and consequently, distorted lens. It is my hope that this chapter offers some degree of clarification or, at least, inspiration for the reader to investigate such issues more deeply on his or her own.

~

"Throughout Jesus' teaching these two
words *know* and *do* occur constantly, and always in that
order. We cannot do until we know, but we can know
without doing. The house built on the rock is the house of
the man who knows and does. The house built on the sand
is the house of the man who knows but does not do."
Francis Schaeffer; No Little People, Crossway Books, p.28

"My brother, sister, friend: read, study, think, and read
again. You were made to think. It will do you good to
think; to develop your powers by study. God designed that
religion should require thought, intense thought, and should
thoroughly develop our powers of thought. The Bible itself
is written in a style so condensed as to require much intense
study. I do not pretend to so explain theology as to dispense
with the labor of thinking. I have no ability and no wish to
do so." Charles G. Finney Finney's Systematic Theology,
(Bethany House Publishing), Preface, p.2

~

Chapter Two

Hearing, Understanding and Doing

In this chapter, we will consider the relationship between and the importance of *hearing* (being exposed to truth), *understanding* (assimilating the meaning of truth to which one is exposed) and *doing* (acting upon and behaving according to the truth one understands).

Hearing

On a number of occasions, Scripture reveals that simply having certain abilities is not sufficient for producing "good fruit." In order to be fruitful, a particular, proper use of one's abilities is necessary. Scripture often refers to physical abilities of human beings to make a spiritual and moral point. For example, Mark 8:18 records that Jesus said, "Having eyes, do you not see? And having ears, do you not hear?" This indicates that having the ability to perceive truth, they did not, in fact, perceive the meaning and significance of such truth. The prophet Isaiah makes a similar statement when saying, "You have seen many things, but you do not observe them; your ears are open, but none hears" (Isaiah 42:20).

Regardless of what one does with the information presented, the process of consistently producing good fruit *begins* with exposure to truth. This takes place on a number of levels. There are certain truths that are "standard equipment" with human beings. In Romans 1, Paul states, "…that which is known about God is evident within (us); for God made it evident to (us)." God placed a measure of truth within us and all around us as all of creation reveals truth about our Creator. In Romans 2, he establishes that we have "…the Law written in (our) hearts." Unfortunately, Paul also states that we have suppressed this truth and are therefore, without excuse for our immoral behavior and consequent guilt (Ro.1:18-20). He further indicates that even in this state of guilt, the Gentile *can* instinctively do the things of the Law. Paul clearly asserts that sin is not an issue of being void of truth or lacking the ability to respond to available truth, it is a rejection of truth and a refusal to use one's abilities properly. However, when a guilty person does something that is consistent with the Law, it does not relinquish his or her previously established guilt.

Beyond an initial level of communication and exposure to truth, there are deeper levels of moral truth and information presented in Scripture. Truth about God and His provision for and instruction about deliverance from moral guilt and bondage are expounded upon in the pages of Scripture. Paul continues in Romans 10:13-14 by writing, "Whoever will call upon the name of the Lord will be saved. How then shall they call upon Him in whom they have not believed? And how shall they believe in Him whom they have not heard? And how shall they hear without a preacher?" We see, in this passage, a definite recognition that there is a need to **hear** truth before one can benefit. There are two important points to acknowledge in this opening section – exposure to truth is a necessary first-step toward producing good fruit (character and valuable contribution to the lives of others, society and the kingdom of God) and exposure to truth does not automatically produce good fruit; one might handle such truth appropriately or inappropriately.

In reference to hearing and being exposed to truth, we turn our attention to the parable of the seed and the soil in Matthew 13:18-23. Each group represented in this parable was exposed to truth, having seed (the word of the kingdom) sown upon them. This is a necessary beginning in the overall process of moral transformation. However, the first three groups did not respond appropriately to available truth and, consequently, produced no fruit. Jesus offers three general and insightful struggles that can interfere with pressing through to fruitful understanding. Stating, "When anyone hears the word of the kingdom and does not understand it, the evil one comes and snatches away what has been sown in his heart," (Mt.13:19) reveals a basic "heart" (core purpose of life) that is hard and resistant to truth. Next is the challenge of rising above mere selfish reception of truth, having no depth of moral character and virtue to embrace truth for its intrinsic value. Finally, there is the challenge of rising above the value of temporal, earthly, material things to be able to appreciate the greater value of "the word of the kingdom." This corresponds with the statement, "...seek first His kingdom and His righteousness, and all these things will be added to you. So do not worry about tomorrow; for tomorrow will care for itself. Each day has enough trouble of its own" (Mt.6:33-34).

It is important to avoid responding to such revelation as though it is merely another Sunday school lesson that we file away like an old, discarded cell phone in a drawer. We must make personal and contemporary application. For all the exposure to Biblical information church-going people experience, at times it is hard to find evidence that we produce a proper measure of corresponding fruit and personal growth. Without such personal growth on a relatively large scale, we will not experience cultural / national transformation.

Understanding

Again, in this parable, the first group spoken of "...hears the word of the kingdom, and does not understand it...," producing no fruit. However, in verse 23, the parable concludes with "...the one on whom seed was sown on the good soil, this is the man who hears the word and understands it; who indeed bears fruit, and brings forth, some a hundredfold, some sixty, and some thirty." The word "understand" means "to set or bring together," or to "join together in the mind."[17] As we prepare to consider the important role understanding plays in the process of producing good fruit, let us digress slightly to consider the context of the parable.

Jesus is presenting truth *to His disciples.* This truth is presented in such a way that those having a particular level of understanding will gain more understanding while those unprepared for such truth will fail to grasp what is being taught. The understanding in question specifically pertains to the kingdom of God. This is to be seen as part of the training of His disciples; preparing them for their upcoming work. Certain people might feel it is unfair for Jesus to keep truth from some while making it available to a special, specified group. To avoid this tendency, we could think in terms of a sports team. There are times when those who play a certain position on the team (a catcher in baseball or a quarterback in football) will gather for specific instruction or training that pertains to their role on the team. This is not to belittle the other players but to prepare certain people to play their role to the ultimate benefit of the team. On the other hand, we could consider the environment of a classroom. Having gained understanding about certain mathematical principles, some students are prepared for the next level of information while such instruction would only serve to confuse other students. The *next level of information,* referred to above, is not something a good teacher will give to a student not advanced enough to use it properly. Such information will likely produce confusion. Though the context of the parable involves keeping some people from deeper understanding, it is not because God is against understanding but because understanding involves "joining together" new information with information previously grasped in order to produce a

---

[17]Strong, J., Strong's Exhaustive Concordance (Ontario: Woodside Bible Fellowship).

broader, more comprehensive perspective. Thus, certain information depends upon prior understanding before it is appropriate to dispense. This is certainly the case regarding the truths and principles of God's kingdom and His purposes in and relationship with planet earth and human history. I am convinced that God wants us to gain as much understanding as possible and produce as much fruit as possible, recognizing that such understanding proceeds "...order on order, order on order, line on line, line on line, a little here, a little there."[18] Consequently, the statement "...whoever has, to him shall more be given..." is to be understood according to the explanation above. Consider, as well, that Jesus taught that the one who is *faithful with little* is faithful with much and to whom much has been given, much will be required. God is good and wise in all He does.

The point of this section is to emphasize that producing fruit involves more than simple exposure to truth. According to the parable under consideration, many people were exposed to truth (the word of the kingdom) but only one category actually produced fruit as a result. As well, of those who gained understanding, some produced "more" fruit than others. It was "...the man who *hears* the word and *understands* it..." who produces various amounts or levels of fruit. This would seem to suggest that the more understanding one gains, the more fruit one can *potentially* produce.

A number of cautions and clarifications are in order. First, I am not suggesting that *understanding* alone will produce fruit. There are issues such as faith, character, perseverance, wisdom, etc. that factor into this process. As well, I am not suggesting that the possession of an abstract thing called "understanding" automatically produces fruit. I am emphasizing that the process of consistently producing

---

[18] Isaiah 28:10. The verses 9-13 of this passage address this idea in an interesting way and surfaces often throughout Scripture.

fruit includes and involves having and properly using understanding. Understanding refers to the mental process of correctly "joining together" information to expand one's comprehension of truth that is available to formulate in the mind. We might envision a jigsaw puzzle of which we connect the various pieces in order to get the picture. Understanding involves specific mental effort to analyze, reflect upon, reason and logically work with available information. Many people assume that there should be no need to think and, consequently, refuse to make an effort to do so.[19] There is a direct connection between thinking and gaining understanding. Charles Finney wrote, "My brother, sister, friend – read, study, think, and read again. You were made to think. It will do you good to think, to develop your powers by study. God designed that religion should require thought, intense thought, and should thoroughly develop our powers of thought. The Bible itself is written in a style so condensed as to require much intense study. Many know nothing of the Bible or of religion because they will not think and study. I do not pretend to so explain theology as to dispense with the labor of thinking. I have no ability and no wish to do so."[20]

While considering the mental processes related to assimilating truth, a distinction between knowing, understanding and wisdom might prove helpful.

Those able to identify the engine of a car have knowledge. Those who can offer a technical explanation of the operations of a combustion engine possess understanding. Wisdom involves the mental process of

---

[19] Sadly, many professing Christians create a dichotomy between thinking and being spiritual, assuming that using our God-given mental abilities in a thorough manner is contrary to trusting or having faith in God, that we are simply to expect the Spirit to pop revelation into our minds.
[20] Charles G. Finney; Finney's Systematic Theology, (Bethany House Publishing), Preface, p.2

envisioning the practical application and useful function of such an engine. Wisdom involves identifying the best means of arriving at the best end.

Illustration

Walking along the sidewalk near the edge of town, you notice a man standing on the train track as an incoming train approaches from behind.

Scenario 1: Knowing you are close enough to get his attention were you to shout, you quietly stand and watch, thereby giving the endangered individual no warning. Hearing no truth about his impending doom, he does nothing in response to his dangerous situation.

Scenario 2: Knowing you are close enough to get his attention were you to shout, you raise your voice and shout a number of indistinguishable words and phrases in a combination of various languages that the individual is not able to understand.

Scenario 3: Knowing you are close enough to get his attention were you to shout, your raise your voice and shout a very clear and appropriate warning that the individual hears and understands with absolute certainty. With full awareness of the clear and present danger, he maintains his current position, refusing to budge.

In each scenario above, the impending doom of the oncoming train is not averted. Hearing no truth or warning, there is no reason to change one's position. Hearing something that one does not understand (for whatever reason), there is no reason to change one's position. Gaining understanding but refusing to act upon and obey the truth made known, one suffers the consequence of rebellion and stubbornness. With this, we can briefly consider the importance of obedience to known truth.

To this point, I have emphasized the importance of being exposed to truth and of gaining understanding of the truth to which one is exposed. We must deal with the idea that simply because large numbers of people gather in buildings to hear sermons week after week, it is not safe to conclude that they walk out of the building with understanding. If they have understanding, there is no guarantee that they will practice obedience. We proceed to consider the role of obedience in producing good, lasting fruit.

Obedience

Hearing (exposure to) truth is important. Understanding the truth one hears is, as well, very important. To complete the circuit and produce fruit, obeying or acting upon the understanding one gains is crucial.

I would like to begin this consideration by suggesting that a poor understanding and representation of the topic of "works" *has often* discouraged obedience. It is common among certain Christian communities to emphasize that we are not saved by works. This is *frequently* communicated in such a way that one might get the impression that behavior and obedience *are* unimportant or *they are a* form of self-righteousness to be avoided at all cost. This flows from failing to understand Paul's references to "works of the law" in their correct, 1st century, Jewish context. It is not obedience to which Paul is opposed but, rather, the effort of a guilty sinner to achieve and maintain right relationship with God by way of the external religious rituals practiced by devout, orthodox Jews. I would also like to clarify, as we prepare to consider a number of passages of Scripture, that I am not encouraging obedience that produces salvation but, rather, salvation that produces obedience.

A further clarification relates to the fact that not all obedience is manifest from a right motive of heart. When dealing with young people I have often presented a scenario involving three siblings interrupted by their mother as they watch television, asking them to carry the groceries from the car into the kitchen. One responds by carrying groceries (obedience) while grumbling and complaining about his mother having interrupted his entertainment with her request. Another carries groceries (obedience) because she thinks it will increase the chances of her mother allowing her to go to a movie with friends. The third recognizes and appreciates the hard work of her mother to earn money and spend it shopping for groceries to share with them and therefore, gladly carries the groceries (obedience) even putting them away. All three were obedient but only one acted out of love. It is important to emphasize that Christianity involves obedience preceded by or as a manifestation of love.

In Matthew 7:24, it is recorded that Jesus stated, "…everyone who hears these words of Mine, and acts upon them, may be compared to a wise man…" It is not sufficient to simply hear, or even understand the teaching of Jesus. To produce the fruit of a changed life and the fruit of righteousness (Ep.5:9, Phil.1:11, He.12:11 and Jms.3:18), one must act upon, do, practice or obey His teaching.[21]

To produce good fruit and press on to maturity, obedience is the necessary response to the truth one understands. Christianity is not simply a matter of

---

[21] It might be said that the essence of the teaching of Jesus is instruction on how to live a life of love. I am speaking of the well-rounded, challenging, self-sacrificial, sensitive, confrontational, highest-good-seeking love largely misunderstood by the vast majority of people. I am not referring to the warm, fuzzy concept of love that many assume.

intellectual assent to a body of information. It involves an obedient relationship to the Head of the Church, Jesus Christ. Hebrews 5:9 states, "...having been made perfect, He became to all those who obey Him the source of eternal salvation..." This implies that obedience plays an important role in one's salvation, challenging the improper emphasis of the "we're not saved by works" doctrine.

None of these steps are automatic. If one does not make an effort to become exposed to increased amounts and deeper levels of truth, it will not necessarily happen. If one does not think, reason and employ logic, analyzing what they've heard, it does not automatically produce understanding. Obedience requires effort, discipline and self-control.

Scriptural Reflection

Romans 1:18-21 – Truth is available. Suppressing truth produces a variety of negative consequences.

Matthew 13:19-23 – Only those who understand the word of the kingdom produce fruit.

Matthew 7:24-27 – Hearing truth and acting upon it produces stability.

Romans 10:13-15 – Preaching (teaching, proclaiming) truth is an important part of the process that leads to salvation.

Matthew 13:13 – Many people have been exposed to sufficient truth and yet do not understand and, consequently, do not obey it.

Romans 1:31 – Lack of understanding is characteristic of those living in rebellion.

Matthew 5: 21, 27, 33, 38 & 43 – The Jewish people were exposed to great truth and yet twisted and distorted it.

Ephesians 4:17-19 – Once hearing and understanding truth, we are not to "walk" (live, conduct ourselves) as we once did.

James 4:17 "…to one who knows the right thing to do, and does not do it, to him it is sin."

Proverbs 22:17 "Incline your ear and hear the words of the wise, and apply your mind to my knowledge…"

Proverbs 1:5 "A wise man will hear and increase in learning, and a man of understanding will acquire wise counsel…"

Conclusion

As moral agents, created in the image of God, truth plays a crucial role in developing proper character and producing good fruit. In Ep.6:13-17, the apostle Paul states that the first piece of the armor of God is truth and his final reference in this illustration is to the sword of the Spirit, the word of God ("Your word is truth" – Ps.119:160, Jn.17:17). One must use their God-given mental capacities to properly assimilate and understand truth. Once truth is understood, we must obey and live according to it if we are to "…bear fruit in keeping with repentance" (Mt.3:8).

~

"...the moral quality does not belong to the external act, for the same external act may be performed by two men while its moral character is, in the two cases, entirely dissimilar. Nor does it belong to the conception of the external act, nor to the resolution to carry that conception into effect; for the resolution to perform an action can have no other character than that of the action itself. It must, then, reside in the intention."
Francis Wayland, The Elements of Moral Science, (Boston: Gould and Lincoln), p.30

"Only if moral behavior characteristically involves our interpretation of a situation instead of fixed, mechanical cause-effect, is a path cleared for an interpretation which does involve personal responsibility."
Albert H. Hobbs, Man is Moral Choice, (Arlington House Publishers), p.252

~

Chapter Three

Moral Agency and the Nature of Love

God created human beings in His own image. This is the most important thing we can know about ourselves. What does this mean? A complete answer to this question would require volumes. In this chapter, we will consider a few fundamental ideas about the image of God and the moral agency of man. Our reason for considering these ideas is more than academic. If we are to be fruitful human beings and, as well, help others in this process, an understanding of these basic truths is important. The basic truths of which I refer are truths about the function of and relationship between the Mind, the Emotions and the Will, three fundamental elements of moral personality.

Mind

God created human beings with a mind designed after His own mind. It is the same *kind* of mental function as that of God, though we have never expressed the same *capacity* of mental activity. This amazing ability is often underestimated and taken for granted. We have a God-given intellectual ability to reason, to receive, gain, analyze, process, synthesize and understand information, thereby growing in knowledge. Our minds possess the capacity to see the strange little markings on this page, combine them into words, sentences and paragraphs and translate it into concepts and meaningful information. We do the same with sound waves proceeding from the voice box of another human being. Such information might be basic, "cold" facts or *moral* truth, concepts related to good and bad, right and wrong, virtue and vice.[22]

Emotion

Man's emotional system involves the ability to experience feelings in response to various forms of stimuli. This function is associated with our five senses in conjunction with various forms of mental and physical stimulation. For example, we might hear certain information that triggers anger, sadness or joy. We might experience an event that inspires feelings of jealousy or embarrassment. This can often prove to be a powerful factor in motivating one's behavior in specific situations, right or wrong.

Will

The human capacity known as the will relates to an ability to voluntarily originate purpose and action. This is the powerful and somewhat mysterious ability to make choices. Such choices can be creative and / or responsive. Exposed to an array of thoughts, feelings and influences, the will possesses the capacity to resist or to yield. The will, however, is not something one can place into a test tube and examine. It cannot be seen as a physical entity. We know of its existence due to its activity and usage, as we are conscious of employing it in a wide variety of circumstances and situations.[23] Though there is continued

---

[22] If I were not making a conscious effort to keep this information brief and to-the-point, we could consider functions of the mind such as *imagination* and *memory*. Take a moment to imagine how life on earth would radically change if human beings were utterly void of the capacity to imagine or remember.

[23] Of course, there will always be those who submit that this is but an illusion.

controversy regarding this mysterious ability,[24] the operations of the will are not subject to strict determinism. Though one can succumb to conditioned responses on a significant level, the will, in the final analysis, is free to overcome deterministic and conditioned considerations.

The Relationship between the Mind, Emotion and Will

It is common to think and speak of these three capacities in very individual, independent terms. However, it is very important to be conscious of their intricate relational interaction as we attempt to regulate our moral choices and behavior, becoming healthy, productive human beings that reflect and honor, in contrast to violating, the image of God.

The following consideration is not in reference to which of these "components" acts *first* but which one is designed to govern, regulate or "rule" human behavior. All three play their particular, unique role, contributing to the moral outcome. It is very possible, and unfortunately all too common, to establish an inappropriate relationship between these three capacities of moral agency. Our goal is to arrive at a proper relational order, producing good fruit. However, it is also possible to have a proper relational balance between these incredible abilities and yet use them to serve evil.[25] If we are to function properly, the relationship

---

[24] Not only is there controversy but there is also significant confusion. As the will is central to man's moral nature and accountability, it cannot be subject to strict determinism. Strict determinism would not describe the functioning of the will but rather the elimination of the will.

[25] The purpose of this chapter is to encourage the reader to establish the proper relational arrangement between the mind, the will and the emotions. As stated, one can produce evil while having these three aspects of moral agency in proper order. Whether one produces good or evil is ultimately an issue of one's heart. For more information on this, see the previous book in this series, Change Your Heart.

between the mind, emotions and will must be in proper order *for the proper reason.*

Three Possible Arrangements

Remember, it is not an issue of which acts or functions first but, rather, which is designed to govern or control the outcome in the final analysis. As well, I am attempting to take very complex concepts and reduce them to a most basic consideration, therefore, requesting the reader's indulgence.

Arrangement One: This involves the *intellect* ruling over the *emotions* and the *will*. There are two possibilities associated with this arrangement. We might have intellectual activity stir our emotions after which we yield our will to the emotional impulse, or we might have a thought upon which we act after which we experience an emotional response.

An example of the first arrangement above would be an individual who sees something that stirs **thoughts** of a hurtful experience from the past. As the individual *dwells on the thoughts* generated by this image, he becomes increasingly *angry.* The anger builds until someone makes an unkind remark at which time he surrenders his *will* to the anger generated by his thoughts, engaging in a violent response (manifested in a wide range of possibilities).

An example of the second arrangement involves entertaining the **knowledge** that an acquaintance has a sum of money in a particular drawer. In response to this *thought,* along with *thoughts* about what you could buy with the money, a *willful* decision is made to take it. Having taken it, some degree or dimension of *guilt* (or worse, happiness) begins to operate within the realm of the *emotions.*

Arrangement Two: This involves the *emotions* ruling over the *intellect* and the *will.* This can also happen two ways. One's *emotional* state might produce certain *thoughts* to which one surrenders and *acts* upon or one's *emotional* state might produce *action*, bypassing reason, only to *think* of the behavior later (if at all).

An example of the first arrangement could involve a person having **anger** toward a particular individual upon which his *thoughts* dwell until he commits an *act* of violence toward this person.

An example of the second arrangement could be a person **emotionally** responding to an insult with an *act* of violence, after which *thoughts* of regret plague the mind.

Arrangement Three: The *will* can rule over the *intellect* and *emotions*. We might first consider that one's *will* can rule by governing what the *intellect* concentrates upon, allowing *emotion* to follow the action that is intellectually chosen.[26] The other option is, one *willfully* governs (controls or limits) their *emotions* so that their *mental* activity is not taken over by emotional blindness, producing unhealthy behavior.

Before offering examples of these options, it is important to point out that there are some unique characteristics to this arrangement. First, though one's will can regulate and limit emotions, one cannot willfully *produce* emotions. In other words, though I can *control* my anger, I cannot *directly* choose to *produce* the emotion of anger. To produce actual anger, in contrast to simply *acting* (in the sense of portraying) angry, I must first think about or experience something that produces the actual emotion. I can willfully choose the thought or action that produces the emotion, but this is *indirectly* as opposed to *directly* choosing the emotion.

---

[26] I chose the word "intellectually" as opposed to "intelligently" to indicate that the action chosen is the result of mental contemplation while it is not necessarily a *smart* choice.

The other unique issue involves the will being active in more than one way. We might offer these formulas to clarify: 1) Will governs mind – will chooses action – emotion follows, 2) Will governs emotions – will governs mind – will chooses action – emotions follow.

An example of this might involve a person who has a need for money and knows of a place he can conveniently steal such money. Regardless of the strong desire to take the money, he chooses to consider what is appropriate and refrains from criminal behavior. Individuals are capable of regulating their emotions (an act of the will) and taking control of their thought-life (an act of the will).

Having considered the various arrangements, we will contemplate which one consistent with God's design for properly functioning moral agency and best suited to produce good fruit in a consistent manner.

The Interaction between the Mind, Emotion and Will

For a third time, I would like to state that we are not focusing on which of the three (mind, emotion, will) acts first, we are not investigating sequence of action. I would suggest that the dynamic interaction between them is far too complex to sort out in a convenient manner. As we are bombarded by many forms of internal and external influences, good, bad or "neutral," the mind, the emotions and the will are in a constant state of stimulation. A moral agent is not simply a conglomeration of independent, isolated components, fragmented into parts. A person is a unit, operating in diverse unity, many complex aspects and elements interacting and overlapping to produce character.

Our present concern involves identifying which function of moral personality is designed to govern or rule. I will refer to a helpful illustration that has been offered in this regard. Imagine a tractor-trailer. Consisting of two main components, the tractor and the trailer, it is yet in need of someone to govern it, to operate it. We can imagine the person who operates the rig is named Will. He is responsible for stopping, starting, steering and regulating speed. The component of the rig he has *direct* control of is the tractor. The tractor can be thought of as the Mind. When Will controls the Mind properly, the trailer, viewed as the Emotions, follows in a right direction. All three are operating and performing a particular function. If Will were to fail, in any number of ways, to perform his function as the rig is in operation, disaster looms. However, the role of Will, functioning properly or improperly, is to govern. If the tractor is not governed by Will and simply goes wherever it might tend to go, it will likely produce wreckage. Though the tractor is an impressive piece of equipment with many complex functions, it is not designed to be in control. If the trailer were to take control (known as jack-knife), destruction would likely ensue. This does not mean that the tractor and the trailer are bad, dysfunctional or evil; it simply means that they are not designed to be the governing component. They play an active part in a governing process and, under the guidance of Will, contribute to produce the desired results.

With this illustration before us, we can realize that the affairs of life inspire a wide variety of thoughts and feelings. Some thoughts and feelings are "good," nice or pleasant while others are "bad," nasty or unpleasant. There is often a tendency to assume that it is okay to allow our thoughts and feelings to govern if they are good and pleasant. The fact is, however, though there is significant interaction, in producing moral action, a moral agent is ultimately not to subject his will to his thoughts and feelings, but, instead (as our tractor-trailer example illustrates), his thoughts and feelings to his will.

Before we measure this perspective against Biblical statements, I simply assert that regardless of whether one obeys God, walks by the Spirit, walks in love or disobeys, walks by the flesh and live a selfish life, it requires a willful choice. Certainly, our minds and emotions play a role but apparently a person can *know* the right things to do but not do it (Jms.4:17) or *feel* the wrong way but not yield to it (Ga.5:16-17). I would suggest that this is an issue of how one engages the will.[27]

Biblical Considerations

As we consider a few passages of Scripture, it should be quite evident that one must engage the will to direct the mind and control the emotions.

Nearing the end of his instruction to the Philippians, Paul wrote, "Finally, brethren, whatever is true, whatever is honorable, whatever is right, whatever is pure, whatever is lovely, whatever is of good repute, if there is any excellence and if anything worthy of praise, dwell on these things" (Phil.4:8). The word translated "dwell" is "logizomai" which refers to a mental process of recognizing and thinking upon such things. We cannot assume that our minds will automatically dwell upon such. In fact, there would be no need for this instruction if it were so. In order to "dwell upon" or "think upon" these things, one must willfully choose to direct the mind. Even when the mind (in fact, *especially* when the mind), would tend to dwell upon any number of negative or unproductive thoughts, we are designed with the capability to direct, regulate, govern and control this faculty. This is the power of moral agency under the proper use of our God given will.

---

[27] At this point, a consideration of the incipiency of the will as a noumenal concept is in order: (http://www.libraryoftheology.com/writings/freewill/The_Incipiency_of_the_Will_Harry_Conn.pdf)

"Therefore consider the members of your earthly body as dead to immorality, impurity, passion, evil desire, and greed, which amounts to idolatry. For it is because of these things that the wrath of God will come upon the sons of disobedience, and in them you also once walked, when you were living in them. But now you also, put them all aside: anger, wrath, malice, slander, *and* abusive speech from your mouth. Do not lie to one another, since you laid aside the old self with its *evil* practices, and have put on the new self who is being renewed to a true knowledge according to the image of the One who created him..." (Col.3:5-10). First, in order to *consider* such, one must engage the will to direct the mind in this way. Then, we are to put aside a list of potential emotional dominations. How is this done? It requires that we make a proper use of the will to regulate our emotional activity.

Consider such instruction as, "...flee from youthful lusts and pursue righteousness, faith, love and peace, with those who call on the Lord from a pure heart" (2Ti.2:22). How does one accomplish this? Is it according to the way one *feels*? To the contrary, such instruction is foolish if it depends on an emotional inspiration. Is this pursuit accomplished by *knowing* it is the thing to be done? No, one must employ the will to gain and embrace such understanding, regulating feelings to the contrary (youthful lusts) and produce the action.

As I quote Romans 8:5, I suggest reading through verse 14 and applying the concept here considered. "For those who are according to the flesh set their minds on the things of the flesh, but those who are according to the Spirit, the things of the Spirit." How does one "set their minds"? This is clearly a reference to the way one uses the will. As referenced earlier, one can have the will in the place of dominance and yet use it to regulate their mind and emotion to serve the flesh. However, if one is to live (walk) according to God's design for producing good fruit, the will must direct the activities of the mind and the emotions.

The following passages present us with the option of walking by the Spirit or by the flesh. To "walk by the Spirit" is to "walk in love." To live according to the flesh is to yield one's mind and will to the dominance of one's impulses and emotional activities. Walking in love involves making a willful decision to govern one's thoughts and conduct in accordance with the revealed will of God in contrast to one's emotions and feelings or the desires of the flesh. This is a very important arrangement to understand and upon which to act. This is necessary for the production of a victorious, fruitful Christian life as we receive and live according to the provisions and resources of God, in Christ, under the guidance of the Spirit.

"But I say, walk by the Spirit, and you will not carry out the desire of the flesh. For the flesh sets its desire against the Spirit, and the Spirit against the flesh; for these are in opposition to one another, so that you may not do the things that you please" (Gal.5:16-17).

"Therefore be imitators of God, as beloved children; and walk in love, just as Christ also loved you and gave Himself up for us, an offering and a sacrifice to God as a fragrant aroma. But immorality or any impurity or greed must not even be named among you, as is proper among saints; and there must be no filthiness and silly talk, or coarse jesting, which are not fitting, but rather giving of thanks" (Ep.5:1-4).

The American evangelist and revivalist, greatly used of God, Charles G. Finney, writes, "...love...consists in choosing the highest good of God and of universal being, for its own intrinsic value, in a spirit of entire consecration to this as the ultimate end of existence."

I would like to look at the elements of this statement.

First, "…love…consists in choosing…"

Love dies consist in feeling. Love, as a moral quality, requires choice. Of course, not all choices produce or are a manifestation of love. It involves choice of a very specific sort. Love is not a natural attribute but a moral decision, as God does not command us to have certain natural attributes but rather to make moral choices.

It is the choice of "…the highest good of God and of universal being…"

Establishing the purpose of and pursuing the highest good of God and one's fellowman is at the center of love. This requires wisdom and self-control. One's initial impulsive response in a situation will rarely involve the highest good. Consequently, one must govern emotions and mind in an effort to search out the highest good.

First, we are to aim for the highest good of God. This means we resolve to do what is pleasing to Him, consistent with His truth and guidance. This is based on the fact that He consistently operates in love with greater wisdom than any human being. The phrase "universal being" refers to all others without personal partiality that would lead to exceptions that violate love in the grand scheme. The Biblical statement is, "Love the Lord your God with all your heart and with all your soul and with all your mind and with all your strength (and) love your neighbor as yourself."

We are to make this choice "…for its own intrinsic value…"

"Intrinsic" means true, genuine, real or inherent in contrast to assigned or created (made up). There is appropriateness, built-in value to pursuing the highest good. Pursuing one's personal self-interest or the preference of a "special interest group" will not produce the same value or arrive at the same end.

This is to be done "...in a spirit of entire consecration..."

This corresponds with "ALL your heart...ALL your soul...ALL your mind...ALL your strength." Some assume such a pursuit is impossible. I suggest we view this requirement in light of the following question: "Can you throw a baseball as far as you can throw a baseball?"

Finally, we are to be committed "...to this as the ultimate end of existence."

The goal of operating in love and producing love is the filter through which all of our choices are to be made.

~

(The church) "...is to be about what Jesus was about: aggressively breaking down Satanic fortresses wherever we find them. In people's lives, in families, in churches and in society at large, the church is to expand the rule of God on the authority of Christ by binding evil and setting people free. In a word, our charter is to live out a theology of revolt, throwing all we are and all we have into guerrilla warfare against the occupying army, the tyrannizing powers of darkness. When the church opts instead for a theology of resignation and thus attempts to accept as from God what Jesus fought as coming from Satan, the church exists in radical contradiction to its defining vocation."
Dr. Greg Boyd, God at War, (InterVarsity Press), p.217

~

Chapter Four

Understanding Our Appetites and the Strategy of Our Enemy

Prior to game-day, a professional football team carefully considers the opponents strategies and plays, watching films of previous games in order to be best prepared for their offensive and defensive scheme. In like manner, if military commanders and troupes understand the plans and resources of enemy forces, it greatly increases their advantage. The design of this series of books is to equip the saints. We first need to be equipped to gain *personal* victory over the world, the flesh and the devil. We also need to be prepared to be *workers* with God who do not need to be ashamed, overpowering the gates of hell and advancing the kingdom of God. As Peter instructed us to prepare our minds for action (1 Pe.1:13), this chapter contributes to this process by considering Satan's strategy for defeating human beings in his war against God. We will consider three central texts providing insight into his use of the lust of the flesh, the lust of the eyes and the pride of life.

God, in His great love, is attempting to shape us into people who can enjoy the greatest amount of liberty possible (Jn.8:36; 2 Co.3:17; Ga.5:1). Satan, in his devious hatred for God, is attempting to kill, steal and destroy (Jn.10:10). As part of this strategy, he attempts to bring human beings, loved by God and commissioned to oversee all the earth, under guilt and bondage. We gain significant insight into this strategy when reading 1 John 2:15-17.

"Do not love the world nor the things in the world. If anyone loves the world, the love of the Father is not in him. For all that is in the world, the lust of the flesh and the lust of the eyes and the boastful pride of life, is not from the Father, but is from the world. The world is passing away, and *also* its lusts; but the one who does the will of God lives forever."

"The world" refers to systems and structures of society that have no regard for God's design for life on earth. The philosophies and ideologies behind this approach are powerful influences that might affect the way we act and think. John cautioned the church in his age, exposed to its particular expression of such things, to overcome attraction to and avoid setting their affections upon these enticements. As John commands his readers "do not love the world," he is declaring that we must not be supremely committed to the world, its way of viewing and approaching life. As he learned from his Master, Jesus, "no one can serve two masters" (Mt.6:24). We cannot have a supreme commitment to the world and to the Father. It is simply a natural impossibility to be committed to God *and* that which is against God at the same time.

It is important to recall that Paul refers to Satan as "the god of this world" (2 Co.4:4). He also states that we "formerly walked according to the course of this world, according to the prince of the power of the air, of the spirit that is now working in the sons of disobedience (and) formerly lived in the lusts of our flesh, indulging the desires of the flesh and of the mind" (Ep.2:2-3). The "world," in this sense, is the outcome of Satan's strategy to blind the mind and lead people into bondage and captivity. Each age and culture has slightly different manifestations and expressions, but the source and goal remain the same. When individual Christians, or the church, embrace the ways of the world, we can anticipate negative results.

John proceeds to reveal the "tools" Satan has at his disposal. He refers to them as "the lust of the flesh and the lust of the eyes and the boastful pride of life," adding that this are "not from the Father, but is from the world."

Though this is a relatively simple, straightforward statement, it offers massive insight into the warfare that is raging, often unnoticed or denied, all around us.

Preliminary Thoughts

In preparing to define the lust of the flesh, the lust of the eyes and the pride of life I offer the following preliminary thoughts.

Though we will look at the lust of the flesh, the lust of the eyes and the pride of life separately, we must keep in mind that there are many ways that they interact and overlap to form unique expressions of temptation or bondage. They are not simply three isolated, independent, individual, distinct functions.

Another important preliminary thought involves the word translated "lust" in this passage. John uses the Greek word "epithumia," which is often translated "desire." In a sense, it is a neutral word, neither negative nor positive. It gains its sense of value from the context in which it is used. When Paul states, "But we, brethren, having been taken away from you…were all the more eager with great **desire** to see your face" (1Th 2:17), he is not using the word in a negative manner. However, when John uses it in reference to the **desire** of the flesh, he speaks of desire functioning in a detrimental manner. The negative use of the word "lust" is related to whether the desire governs us, or we properly govern the desire. I will attempt to unpack this thought as I begin to address the lust of the flesh.

The Lust of the Flesh

God designed the human being with the ability to experience certain appropriate desires. Some of these desires are associated with our physical needs. We can associate these desires with appetites, urges and impulses. For example, when the human body needs nutrition, nourishment and energy, we experience an appetite for food or drink. This appetite (desire) is designed to function for our benefit. We, however, must govern (regulate, direct and control) the desire appropriately, keeping it within healthy parameters. As moral agents and subjects of moral government, we are capable of making bad choices. Bad choices related to this desire lead to a type of bondage in which the desire begins to govern us in contrast to our governing the desire.[28] This is the sense in which we use the word "lust." Continuing with the fleshly desire for food, an improper relationship with this desire might lead to gluttony, or it might lead to anorexia.

Other desires related to our physical needs (flesh) are the human sex drive and the desire for emotional fulfillment and for excitement. Properly governed, all such desires serve a good purpose. Improperly governed, they become monsters who exercise "control" over us in a wide variety of unhealthy ways.

God will lead us to a right balance regarding such things while Satan is attempting to pervert and distort these things, using them to lead us into bondage.

The Lust of the Flesh involves the attempt to gain ultimate gratification, meaning & value through sensual experience. Though God designed such desire to play an important role in a healthy human life, it is incapable of providing ultimate gratification, meaning & value. In the religious world of the Old Testament, the distorted manifestation of this desire is associated with the worship of Asheroth (Jgs.2:13; 10:6; 7:1; 1 Sa.2:10).

The Lust of the Eyes

---

[28] It must be stated that there is a willful dimension to this arrangement. The initial willful act of surrendering to such a wrong response to desire leads to the desire gaining more "power" and "control" over the subject but, though the function of the will is reduced (in a sense), it is never eliminated.

The Lust of the Eyes is associated with the attempt to gain ultimate gratification, meaning & value through that which we relate to by way of visual orientation. Desires inspired through visual means lead many to assume that certain material possessions or involvement with that which we find to have beauty will provide a level of self-worth that such things are incapable of providing. Many go after such things "full-throttle," only to remain empty and often suffering with guilt when failing to find the fulfillment they expected. In the religious culture of the Old Testament, this deception has association with the worship of Baal (Jgs.3:7, 8).

God created us with an ability to see and appreciate beauty. The desire for beauty has a valuable place in human experience when properly governed and kept within right parameters. Failure to apply proper control over impulses generated through visual stimulation, however, opens the door to inappropriate behavior and potential bondage. One should immediately see how an improper interaction of the lust of the flesh and the lust of the eyes could cultivate fornication, adultery and involvement with pornography, all of this contributing to our soaring divorce rates and abortion practices. The advertisement industry uses the desire of the eye in a rather masterful way, playing upon and encouraging social materialism. People enter debt having been convinced to make purchases they cannot afford or to use products for a desired result because of attractive images promising to deliver something they usually cannot deliver. The entertainment industry specializes in carefully designed images of men or woman that lure people into certain emotional responses that contribute to the formation of personal or cultural value systems. As well, news organizations can create a visual representation of an event that slants it in favor of their agenda.

Being aware of the subtle or blatant ways the world plays upon the lust of the eyes can help us avoid deception. Sadly, however, our culture has "cozied-up" with such unhealthy departures, labeling them "normal" and making them the status quo. No longer trusting the Word of God or the God who gave it to us, we have no way of measuring where we are with where we should be concerning morality. Feeding on dregs and disposing of their invitation to the marriage supper of the Lamb, people are easy prey for deception and temptation, gladly smiling and joking while finding a momentary thrill in temporal indulgences on their way to the slaughterhouse.

The Pride of Life

In the context of I Jn.2, the boastful pride of life is associated with the attempt to gain ultimate gratification, meaning & value through status & position. An Old Testament expression of this perversion is found in the worship of Molech (Le.18:21; 2 Ki.23:10; Jer.7:30; 32:35). As stated previously, each desire or drive God has given to the human race has a proper fulfillment. Satan, however, uses influences at his disposal to distort and pervert our approach toward such things to produce destruction and bondage. God is not against reputation, success, achievement and status. For example, God told Abram, "I will...make your name great." Such things can be part of a healthy life when kept in their proper place. The issue is *how* we go about fulfilling these areas of life, the value we place on them and the results we expect in the area of self-worth and personal fulfillment. Poorly governed, reputation, success, achievement, status and position become idols that govern us, leading us to operate in violation of God's logical and loving limits.

A Unique Blend

When considering the lust of the flesh, the lust of the eyes and the pride of life in practical terms, we can see the operation of such shaping the personal and cultural approach of many individuals and even nations. In varying proportions, mixed and blended to suit the tendencies of individuals and societies, the distorted, unhealthy role that beauty, alcohol, drugs, thrills, possessions and success play is obvious. Hollow, empty people, often gifted and talented, seek to locate their value and worth in identity shaped by things that have no capacity to serve this role in our lives, a role reserved for God as He leads us to reflect His image and likeness and produce good fruit. With proper character, we learn to govern our basic God-given desires, producing suitable expressions, contributing to the fullness and abundance of life.

I John 2:15-17

There are a number of things worth noting from the text before considering Biblical examples of these desires in action.

Turning to our text, we see that the perverted approach of which we speak replaces our focus on God ("the love of the Father is not in him"). We might say that this is a violation of Exodus 20:3 (Dt.5:7) as we place higher value upon and make something more important to ourselves than the intrinsic reality of God's worth. This is manifest in our conduct even though in theory, we might *say* we love God supremely. This is John's point in an earlier statement in the same letter containing the text we have been considering as he states, "If we say that we have fellowship with Him and yet walk in the darkness, we lie and do not practice the truth..." (1Jn 1:6).

We also notice that this way of proceeding is "not from the Father," is contrary to God's will. Often, in a misguided effort to exult and glorify God, people state that everything that happens is the will of God. It is clear in this letter of John's that there is a way human beings can choose to live that is not from God. On the contrary, "the one who does (is doing) the will of God lives (is living) forever."

The great preacher and man of God, Rev. Paris Reidhead (from whom much of this material is derived), offers this definition for *temptation*: "Temptation is the proposition presented to the intellect to fulfill a good desire in a forbidden way." This means that through some channel, there is exposure to a suggestion to make a choice to satisfy an appetite, desire, drive, propensity and / or urge in a wrong way; through a wrong source, with a wrong substance, with a wrong person, at a wrong time, in a wrong place, etc. He goes on to define *sin* as "the *decision* to fulfill a good appetite in a forbidden way." Sin is not limited to achieving a wrong goal, but *resolving* to pursue the wrong way of fulfilling appetites and desires. For example, someone might see a fifty-dollar bill on my desk, noticing that there is no one else in sight. This could result in being *tempted* to take the money. At this point, they can either refuse to entertain the mental temptation to take it, putting the thought out of their mind or continue to entertain the temptation. If, at some point, they *determine* to take it, they have crossed the line from temptation to sin. After this determination has been made, another person walks into the room deterring their plan whereby they never have the opportunity to take possession of the money. Regardless of the fact that they did not carry out their plan, they are guilty of sin.

Genesis 3:1-6

The third chapter of Genesis offers our first glimpse into the deceptive tactics of Satan and how, when effective, the human mind and conduct can be altered.

"...the woman said..."

A very important thing to notice is that Satan attempts to distort our view of God, which is foundational to everything else. Consequently, he begins with, "has God said," followed by a misrepresentation of what God said. Though Eve, embellishing slightly ("or touch it" – Ge.3:3), navigated this deception, I am convinced it served to weaken her confidence in some measure. This was followed by a more assertive attack on God's credibility, essentially calling Him a liar without overtly stating such when he declared, "You surely will not die!" The next step in this process of attempting to stir suspicion about God's character involves using truth in a twisted, deceptive manner. He uses a statement that actually communicates God's intention to protect the pair from something detrimental, stating it in a way that makes God seem petty and egotistical, wanting to prevent people from having wonderfully valuable experiences. "God knows that in the day you eat from it your eyes will be opened, and you will be like God, knowing good and evil."

"...the woman saw..."

With resolve further weakened, doubt bolstered and the hope that death was not to follow her disobedience, Eve took her eyes off God as she reevaluated the tree. This consideration led to the conclusion that the tree was, indeed, good for food. Interestingly, God never said nor did He insinuate that the tree was *not* good for food; He simply gave a moral command that they were not to eat of it. Aided by **the desire of the flesh**, Eve inched closer to actual disobedience. Next, she concluded it was beautiful, a delight to the eyes. God never implied that it was an ugly tree, and therefore, to be avoided. The inappropriate assumption that we should partake of everything and anything that is beautiful, not subjecting our choices to a moral standard has led to significant destruction. Here we see a wrong approach toward **the desire of the eyes**, encouraging disobedience. Prior to eating from the tree of which God had commanded them not to, Eve convinced herself that the tree was "**desirable** to make one wise." Again, we see desire ineffectively governed, not subject to a moral standard, leading to a justification for disobedience.[29] The ungoverned desire for wisdom is associated with **the pride of life**. Such pride, related to knowledge or wisdom, can even occur in the study of theology.

"...she took..."

Upon the unstable foundation created by this careless (or intentional) response to these basic desires, "she took from its fruit and she ate."

"...she gave..."

With many potential factors of impropriety associated with Eve sharing the "forbidden fruit" with Adam, I simply draw attention to the common way in which those in rebellion and disobedience become a source of influence in the spread of such inappropriate and

---

[29] We see the Hebrew word translated "desirable" in other passages, such as, Ex.20:17, 34:24, Dt.5:21 and 7:25.
- "You shall not **covet** your neighbor's house; you shall not **covet** your neighbor's wife..." (Ex.20:17)
- "For I will drive out nations before you and enlarge your borders, and no man shall **covet** your land when   you go up three times a year to appear before the LORD your God." (Ex.34:24)
- "You shall not **covet** your neighbor's wife..." (Dt.5:21)
- "The graven images of their gods you are to burn with fire; you shall not **covet** the silver or the gold that   is on them, nor take it for yourselves, or you will be snared by it, for it is an abomination to the LORD your   God." (Dt.7:25)

destructive behavior. Paul notes this when stating, "...although they know the ordinance of God, that those who practice such things are worthy of death, they not only do the same, but also give hearty approval to those who practice them" (Ro.1:32).

Matthew 4:1-10

"...tempted by the devil..."

As Jesus actively embarked on His earthly mission, He was led by the Spirit. Most often, being led by the Spirit has very positive connotations. It is, therefore, quite interesting to consider that the Spirit led Jesus into the wilderness *to be tempted by the devil.* He was at the end of a forty-day fast and "...then became hungry..." (I am relatively certain my hunger would have kicked in forty *minutes* into the fast). Satan, "the tempter," began his attempt to distract Jesus from His mission. The first effort involved identifying a "weak" point, in this case hunger, and an attempt to convince Him to *selfishly* use powers at His disposal to satisfy this hunger, to take His eyes off His Father and put them on *His need* (a focus characteristic of our culture and current, pop religion). This is Satan's effort to use **the desire of the flesh** as a temptation. We should understand that satisfying appetites related to the flesh is not always wrong but doing so in violation of God's appropriate parameters is wrong. Jesus was prepared for this deception as He responded, "Man shall not live on bread alone, but on every word that proceeds out of the mouth of God." In other words, "We are to do what God tells us, not what our flesh tells us." Are there ways and times to satisfy the desire of the flesh? Yes, within parameters revealed by the Designer.

Recognizing that Jesus referenced a truth associated with a lesson Israel had learned *when they were in the wilderness* (consider Dt.8:3), Satan decided he had to use distorted truth to deceive Jesus, much like His efforts with Eve. Referencing a statement found in Psalm 91, Satan attempted to get Jesus to commit an unnecessary, foolish act *to prove His importance*. This is a temptation designed to appeal to **the pride of life**. Jesus, again, was prepared. Once more, Jesus recalled a lesson Israel, and specifically Moses, had learned *in the wilderness* (see Ex.17:2 and Dt.6:16). "You shall not put the Lord your God to the test." In other words, "Don't play games with God; don't do stupid stuff with a selfish motive in order to get a reaction from God to prove what a spiritual big-shot you are."

Next, Satan, tapping into **the desire of the eyes**, had Jesus *look* at all He would gain if He would commit allegiance to him. There was no argument from Jesus about the apparent truth that Satan exercised a measure of authority over these kingdoms. Paul refers to Satan as "the god of this world" (2 Co.4:4). Jesus responded by declaring that He knew who the rightful Master of man is, referring again to a lesson learned in the exodus (Ex.23:25, Dt.6:13 and 10:20), as He stated, "You shall worship the Lord your God, and serve Him only." At this point, "the devil left Him."

Conclusion

Human beings have two ultimate, potential paths to pursue. "The way of the world" is to live in defiance, rebellion and disobedience to God, dismissing His ordinances in order to fulfill one's appetites any way preferred, assuming it will produce something of significance only to be the authors of death and destruction. This is the mode of operation one produces when one's heart (ultimate goal and supreme commitment) is *not* set on loving, pleasing, honoring, worshiping and serving God. As is stated of King Rehoboam, "He did evil because he did not set his heart to seek the LORD" (2 Chron.12:14). We can consider the other path as "the way of the kingdom." This path leads followers to produce righteousness, right relationships and the fruit of the Spirit. In order to walk this path and produce these results, one learns to govern their God-given appetites, keeping them within healthy, proper parameters. This is the result of having one's heart completely committed to living a life of humble obedience to God, receiving His grace and empowerment to rise above and overcome the world, the flesh and the devil. In 2 Chronicles 16:9 we read, "...the eyes of the LORD move to and fro throughout the earth that He may strongly support those whose heart is completely His." The governing of one's appetites is inherent in the commands and instructions of Scripture. To produce positive results involves a synergism in which God is an active agent and provider while human beings play an active role, cooperating with God and honoring His design for us as moral agents. The following two passages are representative of this arrangement.

"...lay aside every encumbrance and the sin which so easily entangles us, and let us run with endurance the race that is set before us, fixing our eyes on Jesus, the author and perfecter of faith..." (He.12:1-2).

"Grace and peace be multiplied to you in the knowledge of God and of Jesus our Lord; seeing that His divine power has granted to us everything pertaining to life and godliness, through the true knowledge of Him who called us by His own glory and excellence" (2 Pe.1:2-3).

Victory over the world, the flesh and the devil is available as part of God's redemptive deliverance as "...we are to grow up in all aspects into Him who is the head, even Christ…" (Ep.4:15), wisely navigating Satan's personalized batch (designed just for you and your tendencies) of the lust of the flesh, the lust of the eyes, and the boastful pride of life.

~

"…while He (Jesus) walked this planet, to show that is was possible to resist temptation and defeat the Devil with only the power of the Holy Spirit, the guidance of His Father, and the Word of God, the Lord Jesus used none of His Godhead powers. He laid aside His rights and powers as God to tread this world (Phil.2:5-8; Lk.2:52; He.5:7-9) although His essential nature as God remained unchanged. To be fully 'tempted in all points such as we are', and yet be 'without sin', the Lord Jesus had to become fully human. To make Him out to be unfairly more that this during His brief stay on Earth is to miss completely the whole purpose of His life; not only to offer His body as a perfect substitute for our sin, but to show is the way a child of God was to live in this world! (He.2:14-15; 5:5-9) Understand – the Lord Jesus had nothing available to Him on Earth that any child of God does not have available; His Father even arranged for Him to have some disadvantages! (Lk.2:7; Jn.1:46; Jn.8:41) The Lord Jesus was our pattern of true human nature, yet He was 'without sin' (He.4:15) and He 'did no sin'. (1 Pe.2:22) God made human nature; God did not make sin!"

Winkie Pratney, Me of Adam?
(http://www.moh.org/DTM/meoradam.htm)

~

Chapter Five

Increasing

God is a God of increase. Of course, I am not speaking of a selfish, materialistic concept if increase. As moral agents, created in the image of God, we are designed to reflect His likeness, His moral character. However, having violated and dishonored His image, we are in need of redemption. The incarnate Jesus, among other things, put the Father on display. His life reflected the likeness of God in human form. The redemptive provisions available in and through Him, are designed to lead human beings to do the same. As we cooperate with God's ongoing redemptive activity, we are to experience growth – continual, positive change in our character, moral maturity. This is a significant theme throughout the New Testament. We are to enter and remain in this process of growth and transformation. I know of no one who can truly say they have no further need to improve in their practical reflection of God's character. I know some, however, who make no effort to do so. Below are a few passages referencing the increase we should pursue and expect.

> "Other seeds fell into the good soil, and as they grew up and increased, they yielded a crop and produced thirty, sixty, and a hundredfold" (Mk.4:8).

> "The apostles said to the Lord, 'Increase our faith!'" (Lk.17:5).

> "Now He who supplies seed to the sower and bread for food will supply and multiply your seed for sowing and increase the harvest of your righteousness…" (2Co.9:10).

"...because of the hope laid up for you in heaven, of which you previously heard in the word of truth, the gospel which has come to you, just as in all the world also it is constantly bearing fruit and increasing, even as it has been doing in you also since the day you heard of it and understood the grace of God in truth...so that you will walk in a manner worthy of the Lord, to please Him in all respects, bearing fruit in every good work and increasing in the knowledge of God..." (Col 1:5-6, 10).

"...may the Lord cause you to increase and abound in love for one another, and for all people, just as we also do for you..." (1Th.3:12).

"Finally then, brethren, we request and exhort you in the Lord Jesus, that as you received from us instruction as to how you ought to walk and please God (just as you actually do walk), that you excel still more...for indeed you do practice it toward all the brethren who are in all Macedonia. But we urge you, brethren, to excel still more..." (1Th 4:1, 10).

"For if these qualities are yours and are increasing, they render you neither useless nor unfruitful in the true knowledge of our Lord Jesus Christ" (2 Pe.1:8).

As we study the incarnate life of Jesus, we gain valuable insight into God's intention for proper human character. A simple statement made in Luke 2:52 reveals significant information about the growth process Jesus experienced during His life on earth.

"...Jesus kept increasing in wisdom and stature, and in favor with God and men" (Lk.2:52).

Background

As His family joined the large caravan to begin the journey home after participating in the Feast of the Passover in Jerusalem, the twelve year old Jesus managed to slip away from the chaos, into the nearby temple unnoticed by His parents. Likely assumed to be with relatives, the journey began. Once His parents noticed His absence they returned to find Him with the teachers in the temple. We read, "Then, after three days they found Him in the temple, sitting in the midst of the teachers, both listening to them and asking them questions. And all who heard Him were amazed at His understanding and His answers" (Lk.2:46-47).

A Three-Fold Focus

We can be sensitive to three important factors as we approach this chapter. First, it is important to realize, as already emphasized, that the Christian life is one of growth, increase and constant improvement that we should find to be unending in this life (and likely the next). The assumption that we will arrive at a plateau of growth, whether related to knowledge, conduct or character, is unhealthy, counter-productive and unacceptable. Paul's words in his letter to the Philippians provide a wholesome balance in this regard.

> "...I count all things to be loss in view of the surpassing value of knowing Christ Jesus my Lord, for whom I have suffered the loss of all things, and count them but rubbish so that I may gain Christ, and may be found in Him, not having a righteousness of my own derived from the Law, but that which is through faith in Christ, the righteousness which comes from God on the basis of faith, that I may know Him and the power of His

resurrection and the fellowship of His sufferings, being conformed to His death; in order that I may attain to the resurrection from the dead. Not that I have already obtained it or have already become perfect, but I press on so that I may lay hold of that for which also I was laid hold of by Christ Jesus. Brethren, I do not regard myself as having laid hold of it yet; but one thing I do: forgetting what lies behind and reaching forward to what lies ahead, I press on toward the goal for the prize of the upward call of God in Christ Jesus. Let us therefore, as many as are perfect, have this attitude; and if in anything you have a different attitude, God will reveal that also to you; however, let us keep living by that same standard to which we have attained" (Phil.3:8-   16).

Notice Paul's usage of the word and concept of "perfect," as he states, "Not that I have already…become perfect…," and at the same times urges "…as many as are perfect…" to "…press on…" in order to fully know all that is available in Christ. I believe it is proper to represent this view as saying that there is a form of perfection we are to embrace and maintain on the level of purpose and commitment while there is a form of perfect that we seek to obtain concerning external manifestations of our internal purpose. In other words, we might say that the Christian approach toward life is that we are *perfectly* committed to experiencing any and every change necessary to *perfect* all other aspects of life. There is an aspect of perfection that refers to our commitment and an aspect that involves constant growth, change, purification and improvement.

The second factor we can be sensitive to is that Christianity is not dualistic in nature. The Christian faith is not something separate from "real life," it is an approach toward all aspects of personal, social, spiritual and physical existence. There are various ways we allow dualism to have an inappropriate place in the Christian faith. Some assume that Christians should ignore or neglect that which has to do with the physical or natural world. This misconception views our being "in the world but not of it" as meaning that the spiritual world is good and the physical world is bad. However, we must realize that God created a single reality consisting of both physical and spiritual aspects designed to function in conjunction with one another. Both have value and both can be perverted. Our task is to find and maintain a proper, healthy balance in all aspects of life. Though, in one sense, eternal things have more value than temporal things, we understand that "he who is faithful in little is faithful in much." To find this balance we might reference Luke16:11 & 13. Luke 16:11 says, "If therefore you have not been faithful in the use of unrighteous mammon, who will entrust the true riches to you?" This shows that it is unacceptable to ignore or neglect our stewardship of material, "earthly" things.

The other dualistic error is more practical than ideological. Many who ideologically state their commitment to Christ and His kingdom, instead of rejecting the material realm, spend the bulk of their time "serving" their financial and material well-being. Luke 16:13 says, "No servant can serve two masters; for either he will hate the one, and love the other, or else he will hold to one, and despise the other. You cannot serve God and mammon." We will only insure a proper, balanced relationship with earthly things when viewing them through right relationship with God, seeking **first** His righteousness and His kingdom. In reference to "...all these things...added to you..." (Mt.6:33), we neither reject them as unimportant nor exalt them above God and His kingdom. Therefore, in contrast to a dualistic view of life, the Christian faith encourages, in a proper sense (as there are ways of perverting everything), a holistic approach.

The third factor that will surface as we consider the components of Luke 2:52 is that Christians should strive to be the best in any area or endeavor in which they are involved. It should be the case that Christians aim to "set the pace" in all profession, employment and institutions (religion, family, education, government, science, technology, media, arts, business, etc.). This is due to the fact that we are learning to use our abilities and capacities the way God designed them to be used.

Wisdom

Luke 2:52 tells us "...Jesus kept increasing in wisdom..." This is a reference to the mental activity of Jesus. There is some truth to the idea that an aspect of wisdom is more natural to some people than to others, yet wisdom is a much more involved mental process than this idea conveys. Wisdom implies an application of knowledge and understanding which involves specific intellectual activity. We *study* to gather information and gain knowledge and we think to gain understanding. *Thinking* is the intentional intellectual, mental activity of processing information and knowledge in order to arrive at understanding. Wisdom involves using one's knowledge and understanding to determine the best means of arriving at the best end in any given situation or circumstance. Consequently, it implies having understanding which implies having knowledge but it also implies a creative but useful application of such. Jesus *increased* in wisdom and so can (should) we.

God designed and created the human mind after His own. Human beings have the same *kind* but not the same *degree* of mental activity as does God. Wisdom is pleasing to God and God is pleased to share wisdom (Jms.1:5; Mt.7:11). When reading, "For the Lord gives wisdom..." (Pr.2:6), we should not assume this refers to a "hand-out" as much as a mental process of gaining and applying knowledge and understanding the Lord will lead us through as we use our moral capabilities (the mind being one) to follow Him. Intelligence is pleasing to God. For various reasons, too complex to address here, many people assume that being spiritual and being intelligent are antagonistic toward one another, that a person cannot be both. Of course, the wisdom and intelligence we are to develop must be consistent with, not contrary to, His will. Human knowledge, disconnected from Divine guidance leads to pride (1 Ti.6:20, 1 Co.8:1) and foolishness (1 Co.3:19). The Christian, due to connection with the greatest mind in the universe (God) should have better insight and understanding than those separated from God. This is not automatic, it takes study, reflection and proper application of God-given abilities to grow and increase in this area. Learning to use one's mind according to its design is one very important way we honor God and express our love for Him. Referencing Dt.6:5, Jesus reminded His listeners that "...you shall love the Lord your God with all your...mind" (Mt.22:37; Mk.12:30; Lk.10:27). Volumes could, and have, been written on this topic but I conclude by encouraging the Christian community to realize that we should produce men and women who lead the way in all academic disciplines as we honor God by using the mind He has designed and given us in a manner that manifest our love for Him (and others) in this realm of moral agency.

Stature

Stature is a general reference to the disposition of the physical body. Luke 2:52 states that "Jesus kept increasing in...stature." On one level, we would expect a 12-year-old human body to experience such growth as a natural process. On another level, we must avoid the dualistic notion that seems to suggest the physical realm is of little or no importance to a spiritual person. The entirety of God's creation is to be treated with proper stewardship, our physical bodies being no exception. The physical growth Jesus experienced must be considered in conjunction with the fact that He was a carpenter, He engaged in great amounts and distances of travel by foot and those who witnessed His death on the cross were amazed that a man of His stature (presumably impressive) would die as quickly as He did.

We must consider the care of the physical realm, including our bodies, to be part of responsible Christian (if not human) living. Of course, as with everything, we must put it in its proper place; assign it a legitimate position in a larger value system. In other words, we must be prepared to deal with the issue of relative worth in a reasonable manner. Notice that Paul's statement, "…discipline yourself for the purpose of godliness; for bodily discipline is only of little profit, but godliness is profitable for all things, since it holds promise for the present life and also for the life to come" (1Ti 4:7-8) is not intended to convince us that "bodily discipline" is of *no* importance. He assigns it relative value but value nonetheless. Reasonable eating habits and physical exercise, activity and rest are part of the balance to maintaining bodily, mental and spiritual prowess. The common dualistic thinking of the Christian community (and culture in general) makes it easy to overlook this holistic reality.

Favor with God

As we consider the issue of increase and growth, the assumptions many have about Jesus leave little or no room for growth of any kind. The fact of His Divinity might lead some to assume He has no need for such growth. Yet, the statement we are examining in Lk.2:52 makes the amazing claim that "Jesus kept increasing in…favor with God." Our goal, in this section, is to gain insight into growth we should expect to experience as human beings. The human experience of Jesus was genuine and, as such, sheds meaningful light on the realities we can expect as human beings. However, before considering the application in reference to our own experience, I would simply suggest the reader reflect upon the significance of this statement in reference to Jesus, Himself. The idea that He increased in favor with God is quite amazing. The word "favor," is "charis" from which we derive charisma or charismatic, related to grace or gifts. At the very least, this implies that His responses to the experiences and challenges of life were free to be favorable or unfavorable in God's sight. In His human experience, as in ours, receiving God's provision to face each challenge and opportunity produces growth; increases favor with God.

This area of growth is related to spiritual growth and ongoing, proper relationship and interaction with God. Ours is a culture that does not emphasize spiritual sensitivity. Most people experiencing genuine conversion and regaining intentional access to the spiritual realm are extremely immature at the point of entering this new life. Unless there are specific efforts and disciplines pursued to encourage spiritual growth, it is likely that we simply remain immature. As stated about the experience of Jesus, giving proper attention to this area of human life should result in our increasing in favor with God.

Favor with Man

As the Apostle Paul said, "If possible, so far as it depends on you, be at peace with all men" (Rom 12:18). It is clear that we cannot control how people respond to us but as we seek to live righteous lives and speak the truth in love, we should aim to have the best possible relationships we can, all things wisely considered. It is interesting that

Lk.2:52 states that "Jesus kept increasing in...favor with...men." It is clear, when examining Biblical revelation about His life, that this is not a dreamy, pie-in-the-sky concept indicating that He never encountered confrontation, challenges and opposition. We can see that as Jesus lived and ministered, the general response He inspired was favorable. Interestingly, the unfavorable responses largely came from misguided or proud religious people. Jesus provides a balanced pattern to which we should aspire. He did not say or do things merely intended to aggravate people nor did He refuse to do or say that which, though it might aggravate people, was important and proper for them to hear. From this passage in Luke, we see that relationships with both God and man are important and yet we must understand that as we ultimately seek to be pleasing to God, relationship with man must remain subordinate. Though subordinate, human relationships are not to be neglected or thought of as unimportant. As we emphasize the holistic nature of a balanced human life, we must avoid the error of dualism that can lead to the assumption that giving attention to the spiritual aspect of life is important while the physical, earthly or social dimension is of no value. As we pursue a well-rounded approach toward love, we must do what we can to cultivate healthy social lives.

Statements by the apostle Paul, which might seem contradictory are actually expressions of such balance. Consider the following as we attempt to avoid operating in inappropriate and unhealthy extremes.

> "Whether, then, you eat or drink or whatever you do, do all to the glory of God. Give no offense either to Jews or to Greeks or to the church of God; just as I also please all men in all things, not seeking my own profit but the profit of the many, so that they may be saved." (1Co.10:31-33)

"For am I now seeking the favor of men, or of God? Or am I striving to please men? If I were still trying to please men, I would not be a bond-servant of Christ." (Gal.1:10)

"Slaves, in all things obey those who are your masters on earth, not with external service, as those who merely please men, but with sincerity of heart, fearing the Lord. Whatever you do, do your work heartily, as for the Lord rather than for men..." (Col 3:22-23)

"...just as we have been approved by God to be entrusted with the gospel, so we speak, not as pleasing men, but God who examines our hearts." (1Th.2:4)

The point of this chapter is well summed up in Mark 12:30-31 which states, "'...you shall love the Lord your God with all your heart (spiritual), and with all your soul (spiritual), and with all your mind (mental), and with all your strength (physical).' The second (commandment) is this, 'You shall love your neighbor as yourself (social). There is no other commandment greater than these.'"

Made in the USA
Middletown, DE
14 September 2022

10438247R00050